A shoal of fish.

fish

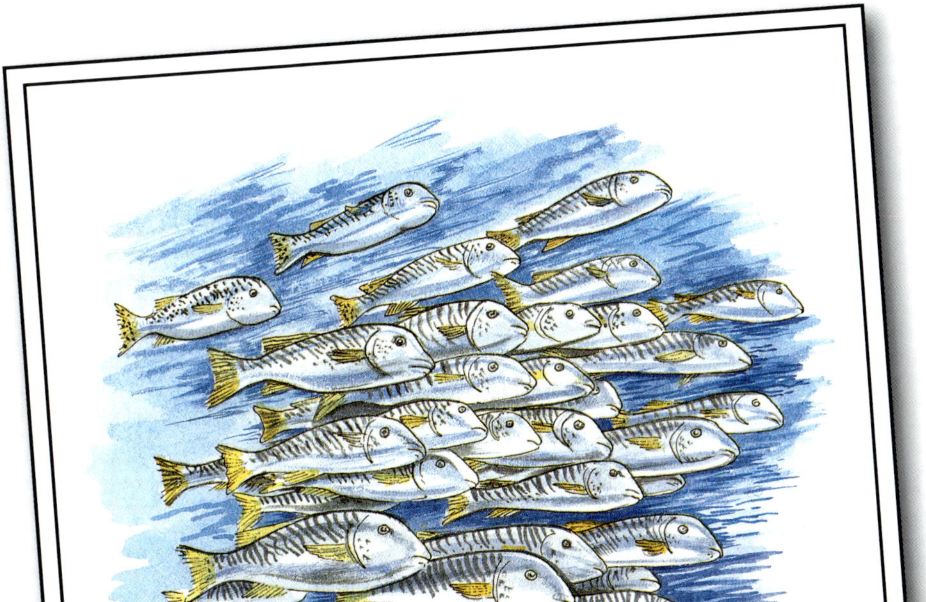

A flock of sheep.

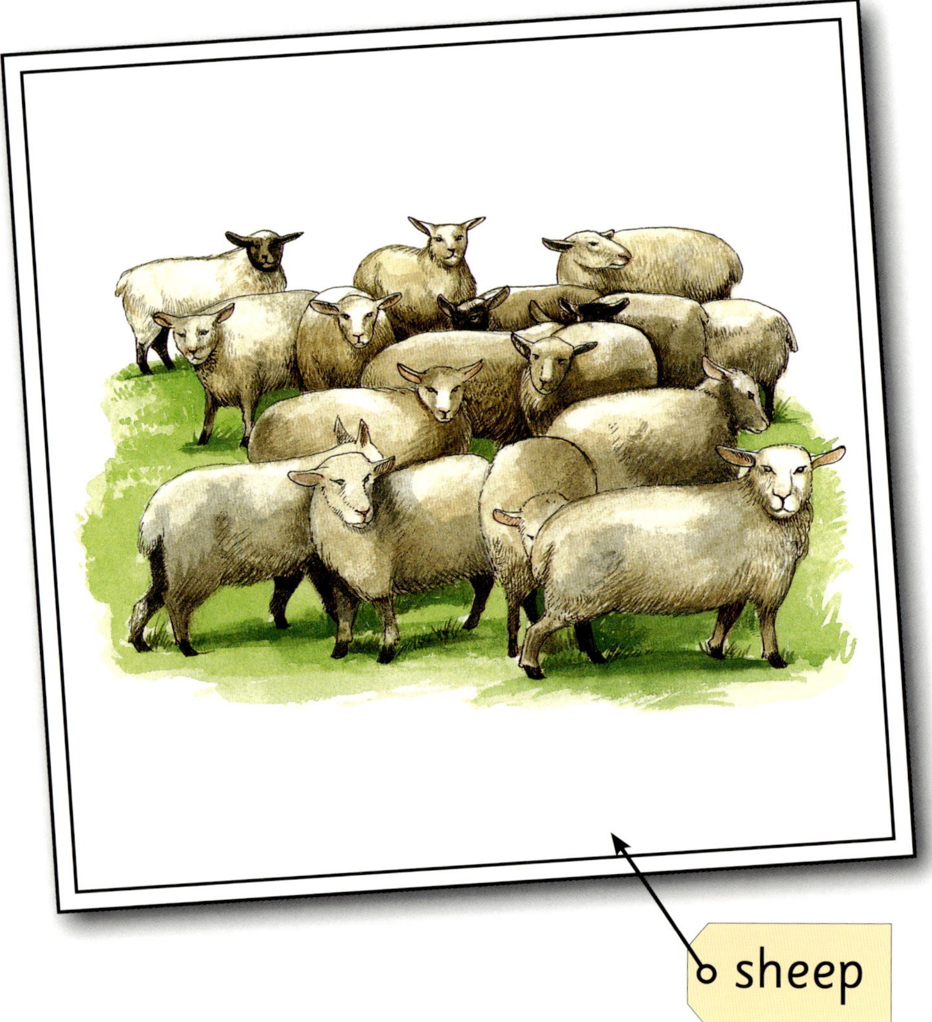

A herd of goats.

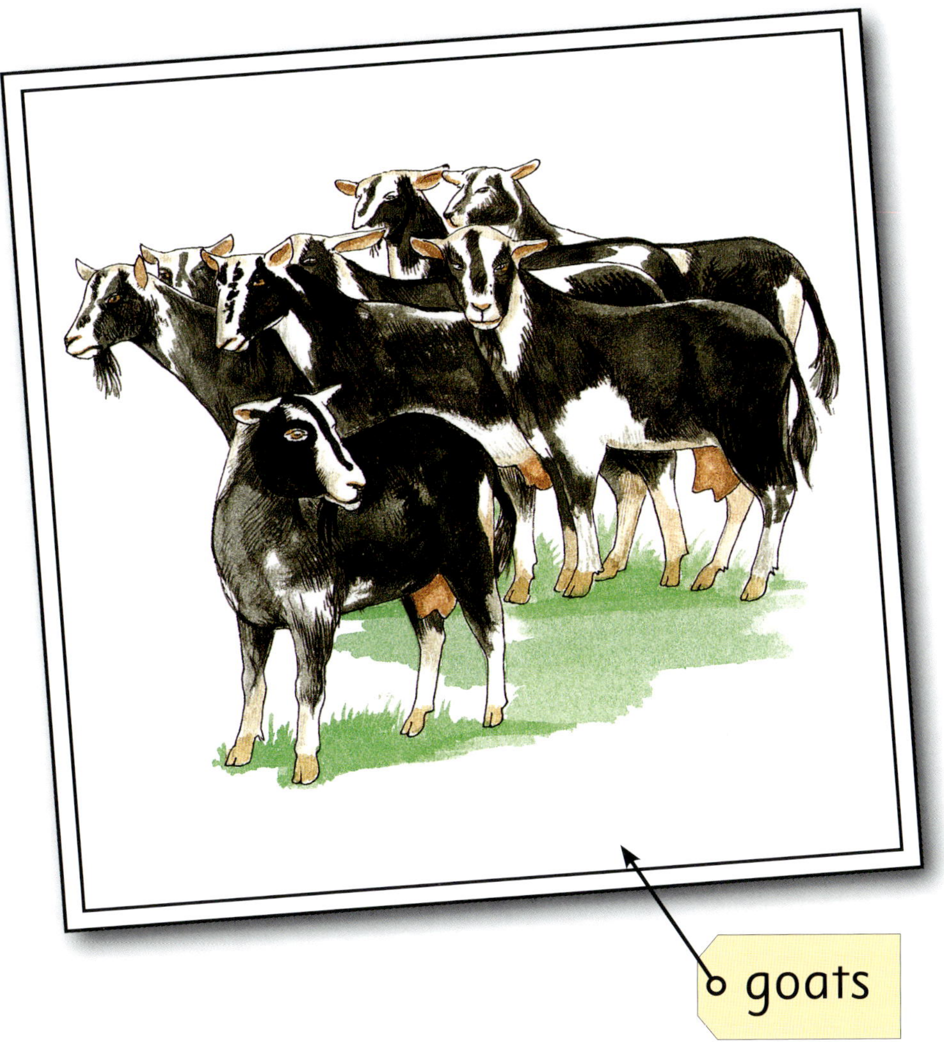

A pack of dogs.

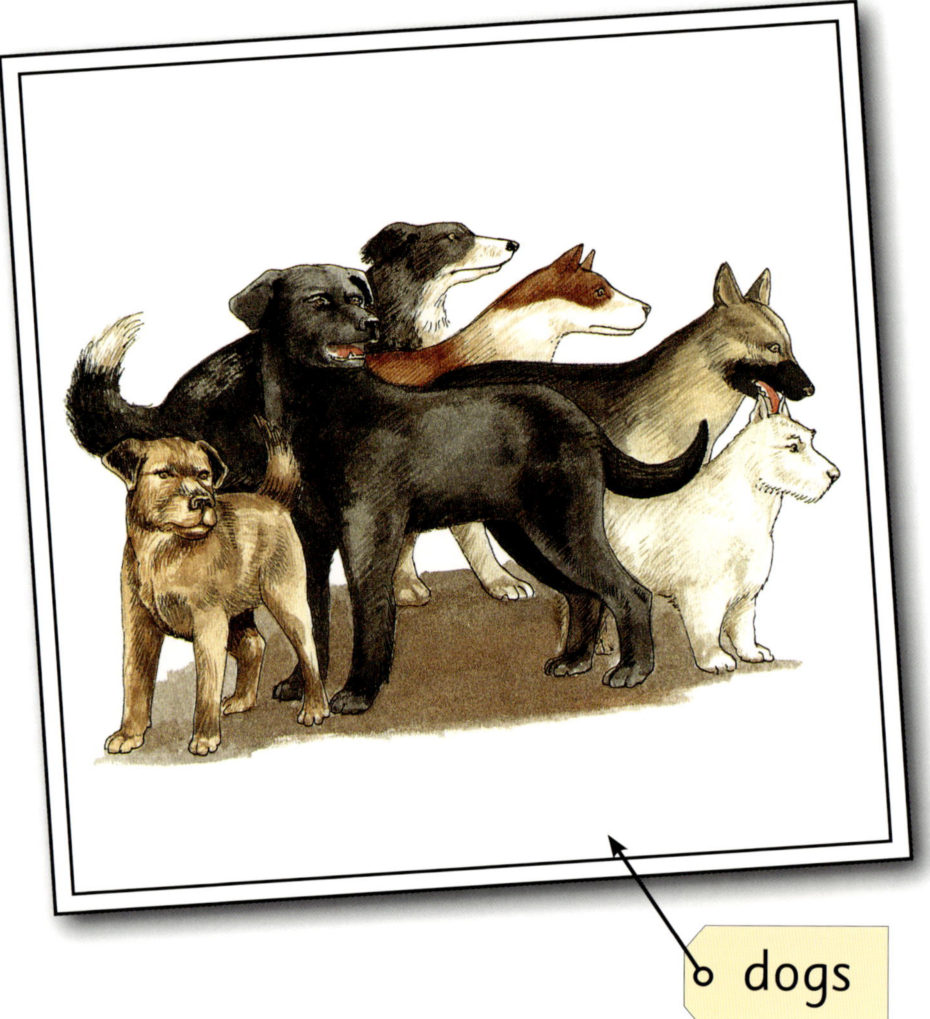

dogs

A litter of kittens.

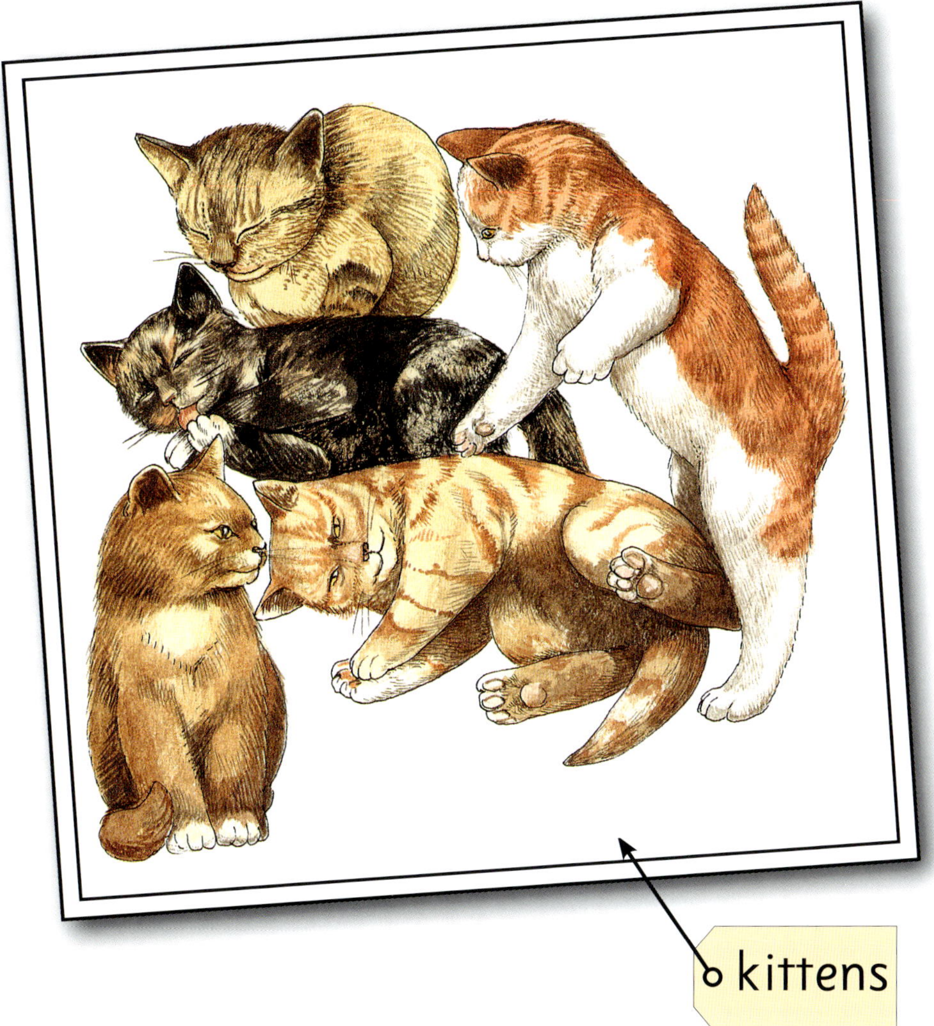

A troop of kangaroos.

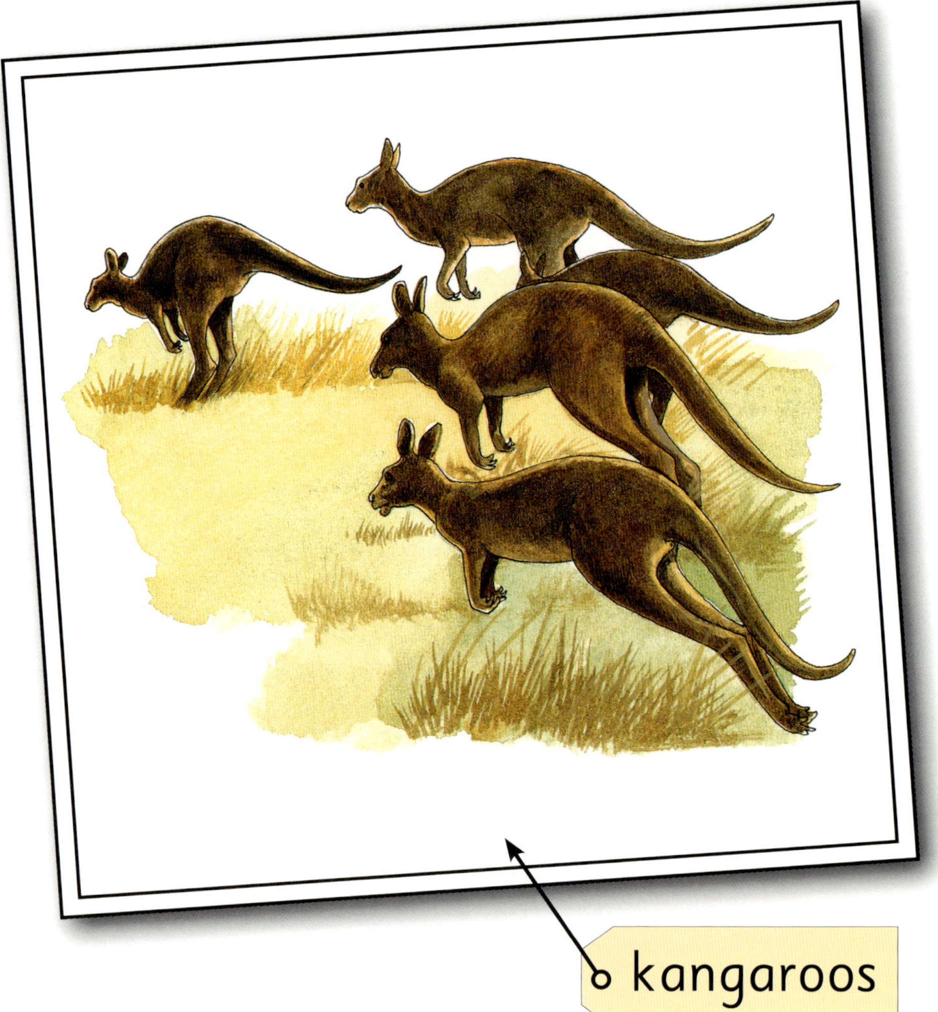

kangaroos

A skulk of foxes...

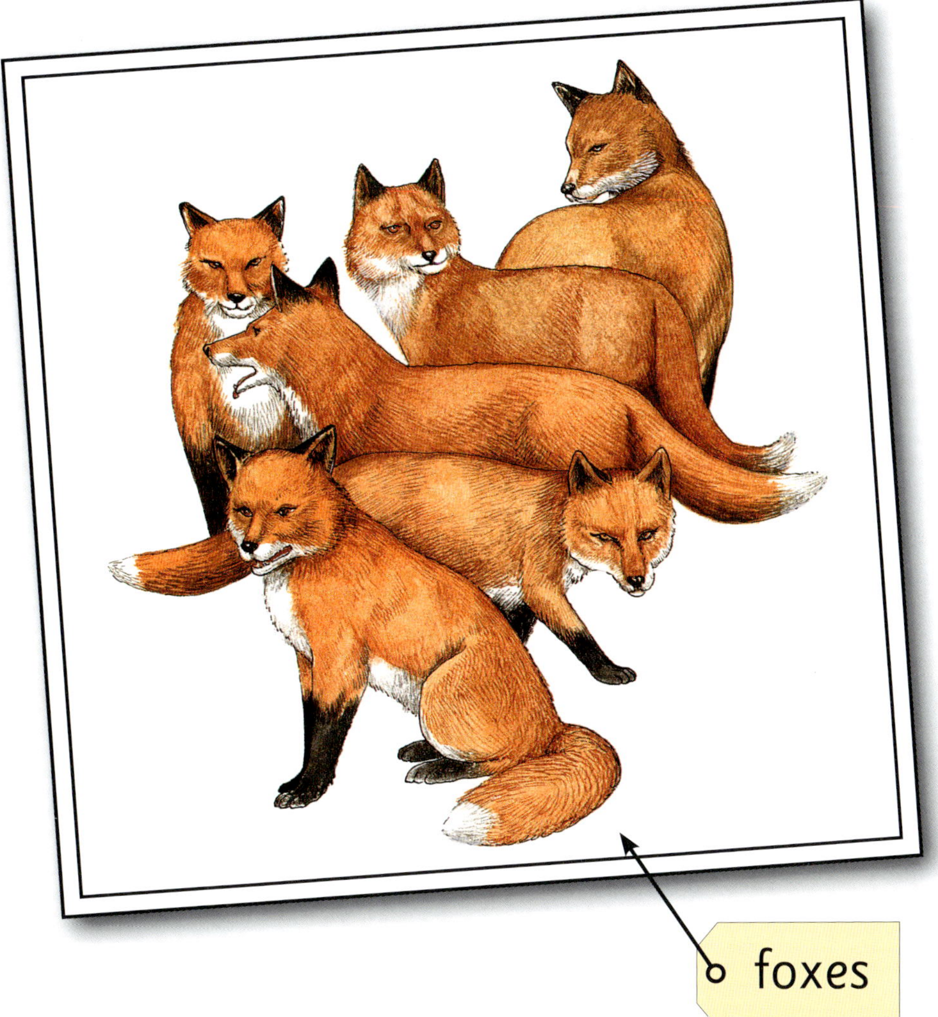

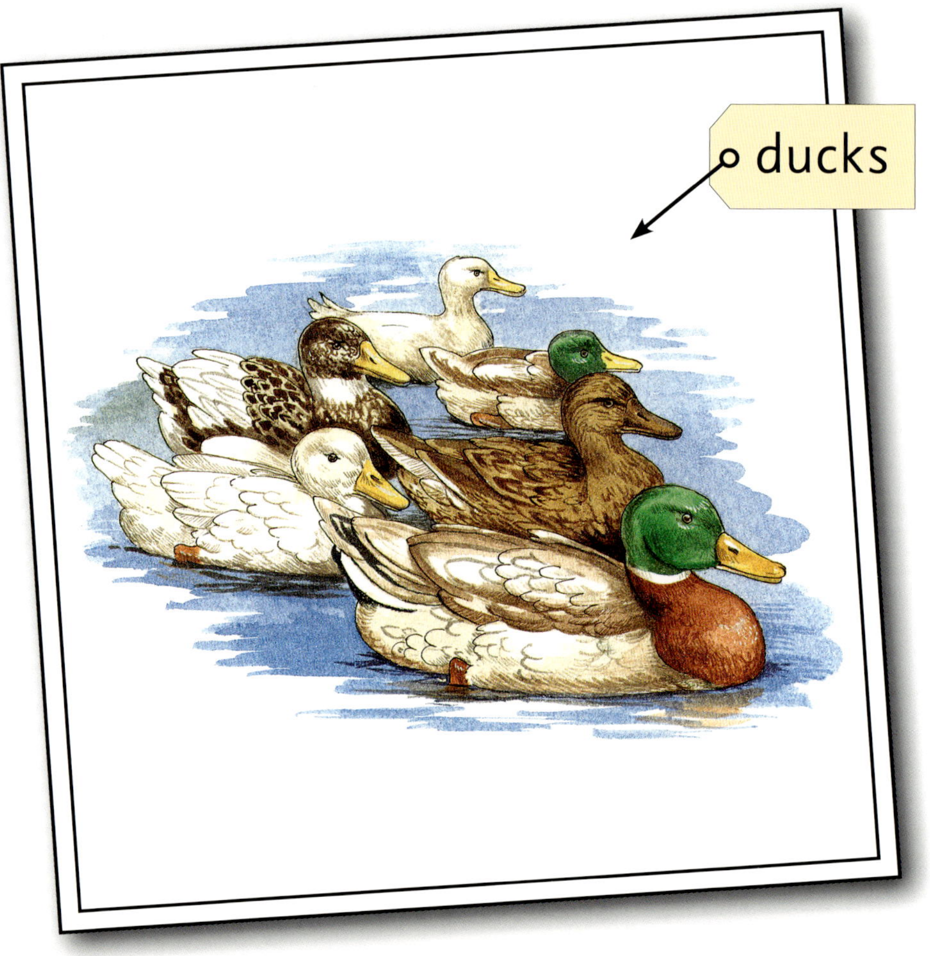

...and a paddling
of ducks!